LACTOSE INTOLERANCE COOKBOOK

MAIN COURSE – 80 + Lactose Intolerance Breakfast, Main Course, Dessert and Snacks Recipes

TABLE OF CONTENTS

BREAKFAST 7

BREAKFAST POWER SMOOTHIE 7

HOMEMADE GRANOLA 8

MACADAMIA PORRIDGE 9

PUMPKIN BREAD 10

FRUIT MUESLI 11

QUINOA PORRIDGE 13

MORNING MUFFINS 14

GRAPEFRUIT & PISTACHIO SALAD 15

EGG & TOMATO BAPS 16

PANCETTA PIPERADE 17

VEGGIE BREAKFAST BAKES 19

PEANUT BUTTER & BANANA TOAST 20

BAKED EGG & CHIPS 21

ASPARAGUS WITH BOILED EGGS 22

GRAPEFRUIT & APRICOT SALAD 23

PUMPKIN WAFFLES 24

SUNBUTTER AND JELLY SMOOTHIE 25

MORNING STRAWBERRY SHAKE 26

FRENCH TOAST 27

AVOCADO KALE BOWL 28

LUNCH 30

RICE PAPER ROLLS 30

CHICKEN NOODLE SALAD 31

SHREDDED SWEET POTATO HASH BROWNS 32

SPAGHETTI WITH MEATBALLS	34
BEAN SOUP	35
HOMEMADE CHICKEN NUGGETS	36
GRILLED VEGETABLES	37
PORK KEBABS	38
TUNA PASTA SALAD	40
ROASTED CHICKPEAS	41
MEDITERRANEAN GRILLED EGGPLANT SALAD	42
BAKED SALMON WITH ALMOND FLAXSEED CRUMBS	43
COLESLAW WITH TERIYAKI CHICKEN	44
TOMATO SOUP	46
CHICKEN EGG DROP SOUP	47
INDIAN KEBABS	48
BUTTERNUT SQUASH SOUP	49
ROASTED GARLIC	50
TURMERIC FRIED EGG	51
FAJITAS WITH BASIL SAUCE	52
DINNER	**54**
POT ROAST	54
ROSEMARY GRILLED LAMB CHOPS	55
ORANGE GLAZED HAM	56
ROAST LEG OF LAMB	58
MUSHROOM PIZZA	59
GRAIN FREE FAJITAS	60
FISH TACOS	62
AVOCADO SANDWICH	63

APPLE ROASTED PORK CHOPS	65
ROASTED EGGPLANT	66
SPINACH SPREAD	67
LENTIL HUMMUS	69
LEMON ROSEMARY CHICKEN	70
SHRIMP SKEWERS WITH GARLIC	71
PICKLED BEETS	72
AVOCADO DIP	73
GREEN BEANS WITH MUSHROOMS	74
BUTTERNUT SQUASH WITH APPLES	76
MEAT MARINADE	77
RED QUINOA	78
SNACKS & DESERT	**80**
ACAI SMOOTHIE	80
PROTEIN SMOOTHIE	81
GOJI SMOOTHIE	82
AVOCADO BLUEBERRY SMOOTHIE	83
VEGAN SHAKE	84
PEACH SMOOTHIE	85
MANGO SMOOTHIE	86
PINEAPPLE SMOOTHIE	87
BEERY SMOOTHIE	88
STRAWBERRY SMOOTHIE	89
BLUEBERRY DESSERT	90
BANANA BREAKFAST CAKES	91
CHERRY PEACH BOATS	93

CARROT CAKE	94
CHINESE ALMOND COOKIES	95
PAPAYA MIX	96
SUGAR CANE JUICE	97
FRUIT SALSA	98
CRANBERRY SORBET	99
CANDY GRAPES	100

Copyright 2018 by Noah Jerris - All rights reserved.

This document is geared towards providing exact and reliable information in regards to the topic and issue covered. The publication is sold with the idea that the publisher is not required to render accounting, officially permitted, or otherwise, qualified services. If advice is necessary, legal or professional, a practiced individual in the profession should be ordered.

- From a Declaration of Principles which was accepted and approved equally by a Committee of the American Bar Association and a Committee of Publishers and Associations.

In no way is it legal to reproduce, duplicate, or transmit any part of this document in either electronic means or in printed format. Recording of this publication is strictly prohibited and any storage of this document is not allowed unless with written permission from the publisher. All rights reserved.

The information provided herein is stated to be truthful and consistent, in that any liability, in terms of inattention or otherwise, by any usage or abuse of any policies, processes, or directions contained within is the solitary and utter responsibility of the recipient reader. Under no circumstances will any legal responsibility or blame be held against the publisher for any reparation, damages, or monetary loss due to the information herein, either directly or indirectly.

Respective authors own all copyrights not held by the publisher.

The information herein is offered for informational purposes solely, and is universal as so. The presentation of the information is without contract or any type of guarantee assurance.

The trademarks that are used are without any consent, and the publication of the trademark is without permission or backing by the trademark owner. All trademarks and brands within this book are for clarifying purposes only and are the owned by the owners themselves, not affiliated with this document.

Introduction

Lactose intolerance recipes for personal enjoyment but also for family enjoyment. You will love them for sure for how easy it is to prepare them.

BREAKFAST

BREAKFAST POWER SMOOTHIE

Serves: *1*

Prep Time: *10* Minutes

Cook Time: *10* Minutes

Total Time: *20* Minutes

INGREDIENTS

- 1 cup silken tofu
- ½ banana
- ¼ cup orange juice
- ½ cup honey
- 1 scoop protein powder
- 2/4 cup strawberries
- 1 cup ice

DIRECTIONS

1. In a blender add all ingredients and blend until smooth
2. Add ice and serve

HOMEMADE GRANOLA

Serves: **2**

Prep Time: **10** Minutes

Cook Time: **30** Minutes

Total Time: **40** Minutes

INGREDIENTS

- 4 cup oats
- 1 tsp vanilla
- ¼ cup water
- 1 cup pitted dates
- 1 cup cranberries
- 1 cup wheat germ
- ¼ sunflower seeds
- 1 cup flaxseeds
- 1 tsp cinnamon
- 2/4 cup honey
- ¼ cup canola oil

DIRECTIONS

1. **Preheat oven to 325 F**

2. Ina bowl mix all ingredients and microwave for 1-2 minutes
3. Add vanilla and water and spread onto a baking sheet
4. Bake for 30 minutes, remove from oven and cool

MACADAMIA PORRIDGE

Serves: **1**

Prep Time: **10** Minutes

Cook Time: **30** Minutes

Total Time: **40** Minutes

INGREDIENTS

- ½ cup raw macadamia nuts
- ½ cup maple syrup
- pinch cinnamon
- ½ tsp vanilla extract
- ¼ apple
- 1 tablespoon wild rice

DIRECTIONS

1. In a food processor pulse apple and transfer to a bowl
2. Pulse macadamia nuts and transfer to the bowl
3. Add the rest of ingredients and mix, top with coconut and serve

PUMPKIN BREAD

Serves: **8**

Prep Time: **10** Minutes

Cook Time: **60** Minutes

Total Time: **70** Minutes

INGREDIENTS

- 2/3 lb. peeled pumpkin
- 5 tablespoons honey
- 2/3 cup sultanas
- 1 cup self-raising flour
- 1 tsp allspice
- 1/3 cup low-salt margarine
- 1 tablespoon pumpkin seeds

DIRECTIONS

1. Preheat oven to 325 F
2. Boil the pumpkin for 10-12 minutes or until tender, remove and mash
3. Add sultanas, honey and beat well
4. Sift the white flour and all spice into a bowl
5. Add the spiced pumpkin mixture and beat well, sprinkle with pumpkin seeds
6. Bake for 55-60 minutes or until golden brown
7. Remove and serve

FRUIT MUESLI

Serves: **6**

Prep Time: **10** Minutes

Cook Time: **10** Minutes

Total Time: **20** Minutes

INGREDIENTS

- ½ cup oats
- ¼ cup bulgur

- 1 green apple
- ¼ lb. persimmons
- almond extract
- pomegranate seeds
- 1 cup apple juice
- ¼ cup almonds
- 1 tablespoon sunflower kernels
- 8 apricots
- 8 dried figs
- 3 tablespoons sugar

DIRECTIONS

1. In a bowl mix water and bulgur, cover for 30-40 minute
2. Add the rest of ingredients and fold into the bulgur
3. Add almond extract and refrigerate overnight
4. Serve in the morning

QUINOA PORRIDGE

Serves: **6**

Prep Time: **10** Minutes

Cook Time: **35** Minutes

Total Time: **45** Minutes

INGREDIENTS

- ¼ quinoa
- 1 cup water
- ¼ tsp cinnamon
- pinch salt
- ¼ unsweetened soy milk
- 1 apple
- ¼ cup blueberries
- ½ cup walnuts
- 1 tablespoons maple syrup

DIRECTIONS

1. In a pot add water, cinnamon, quinoa and salt
2. Boil on low heat for 12-15 minutes
3. Add milk and simmer for 10-12 minutes

4. Stir in berries, nuts and apple, cook for another 8-10 minutes
5. Drizzle with maple syrup and serve

MORNING MUFFINS

Serves: **4**

Prep Time: **10** Minutes

Cook Time: **30** Minutes

Total Time: **40** Minutes

INGREDIENTS

- 1 cup oat bran
- 1 tsp cinnamon
- 1 tablespoon brown sugar
- 2/4 cup soy milk
- 2 bananas
- 2/3 cup brown sugar
- 3 tablespoons sunflower oil
- 1 tsp vanilla extract
- 1 egg white

- 1 cup all-purpose flour
- ¼ cup soy flour
- 1 tablespoon baking powder

DIRECTIONS

1. Preheat oven to 325 F and line a 10 cup muffin pan with muffin cups
2. In a bowl mix cinnamon, oat bran, brown sugar and set aside
3. In another bowl and mix remaining oat bran and soy milk
4. Add baking powder, soy flour, cinnamon and mix well
5. Spoon the mixture into the paper cups
6. Bake for 18-20 minutes or until golden brown
7. Remove and serve

GRAPEFRUIT & PISTACHIO SALAD

Serves: **1**

Prep Time: **10** Minutes

Cook Time: **10** Minutes

Total Time: **20** Minutes

INGREDIENTS

- 1 grapefruit
- 1 white grapefruit
- 1 tablespoon nectar
- 1 tsp pistachio

DIRECTIONS

1. **In a bowl mix all salad ingredients**
2. **Serve when ready**

EGG & TOMATO BAPS

Serves: 2

Prep Time: **10** Minutes

Cook Time: **10** Minutes

Total Time: **20** Minutes

INGREDIENTS

- 2 tomatoes
- 1 tsp olive oil
- 3 eggs
- parsley
- 1 garlic clove
- 2 whole-wheat baps

DIRECTIONS

1. Cook tomatoes on low heat
2. In a bowl beat eggs and add seasoning
3. Add garlic and pour egg mixture and cook on medium heat
4. Halve the baps and squash on the tomatoes, cut in half the omellete and serve

PANCETTA PIPERADE

Serves: *2*
Prep Time: *10* Minutes
Cook Time: *20* Minutes
Total Time: *30* Minutes

INGREDIENTS

- 4 oz. pancetta pieces
- 1 onion
- 2 peppers
- 1 lb. can chopped tomatoes
- 3 eggs
- basil leaves
- crusty bread

DIRECTIONS

1. In a frying pan add pancetta and onion
2. Cook for 8-10 minutes
3. Add the peppers, tomatoes, season and cook for 10-12 minutes
4. Crack the eggs and cook for 5-6 minutes
5. Remove and serve

VEGGIE BREAKFAST BAKES

Serves: 4

Prep Time: 10 Minutes

Cook Time: 20 Minutes

Total Time: 30 Minutes

INGREDIENTS

- 3 mushrooms
- 6 tomatoes
- 1 garlic clove
- 1 tsp olive oil
- ½ lb. spinach
- 3 eggs

DIRECTIONS

1. Preheat oven to 350 F
2. In a baking dish place tomatoes and mushrooms
3. Add garlic, seasoning and drizzle oil, bake for 10-12 minutes
4. Place spinach into a colander, pour over a kettle of boiling water
5. Add spinach and crack an egg

6. Bake for another 10-12 minutes
7. Remove and serve

PEANUT BUTTER & BANANA TOAST

Serves: 2
Prep Time: 10 Minutes
Cook Time: 10 Minutes
Total Time: 20 Minutes

INGREDIENTS

- 2 slices bread
- 1 banana
- ¼ tsp cinnamon
- 1 tablespoon peanut butter

DIRECTIONS

1. Toast 2-3 slices of bread
2. Layer banana slices on toast and dust with cinnamon
3. Spread peanut butter and serve

BAKED EGG & CHIPS

Serves: 2

Prep Time: **10** Minutes

Cook Time: **20** Minutes

Total Time: **30** Minutes

INGREDIENTS

- 2 baking potatoes
- 1 tablespoon olive oil
- 1 tsp paprika
- 1 tomato
- 1 egg

DIRECTIONS

1. **Preheat oven to 350 F**
2. **Drizzle oil over potato wedges and sprinkle with paprika**
3. **Roast for 20 minutes or until tender**
4. **Remove and serve**

ASPARAGUS WITH BOILED EGGS

Serves: 2

Prep Time: **10** Minutes

Cook Time: **15** Minutes

Total Time: **25** Minutes

INGREDIENTS

- 1 tablespoon olive oil
- 2 oz. breadcrumbs
- pinch of paprika
- 14-16 asparagus spears
- 3 eggs

DIRECTIONS

1. In a pan heat oil and add breadcrumbs, fry until crisp
2. Season with spices and cook for another 2-3 minutes
3. Cook the asparagus for 4-5 minutes
4. Boil eggs and place boiled eggs on a plate
5. Divide asparagus and scatter over the crumbs and serve

GRAPEFRUIT & APRICOT SALAD

Serves: **1**

Prep Time: **10** Minutes

Cook Time: **10** Minutes

Total Time: **20** Minutes

INGREDIENTS

- 2 grapefruit
- 3 oranges
- 3 apricots
- 1 tablespoon honey

DIRECTIONS

1. Slice oranges, grapefruits into a boil
2. Add the rest of ingredients and mix well
3. Serve when ready

PUMPKIN WAFFLES

Serves: **4**

Prep Time: **10** Minutes

Cook Time: **15** Minutes

Total Time: **25** Minutes

INGREDIENTS

- 1 cup
- 1 tablespoon baking powder
- 1 tsp cinnamon
- 2/3 tsp nutmeg
- ½ tsp ginger
- ¼ baking soda
- ¼ tsp salt
- 1 cup pumpkin puree
- 1 egg
- ½ cup brown sugar
- ½ cup coconut oil
- 1 cup unsweetened dairy-free milk

DIRECTIONS

1. In a bowl mix baking powder, flour, baking soda, nutmeg, cinnamon and salt
2. In a bowl mix eggs, coconut oil, sugar and pumpkin, whisk in milk
3. Fold the wet mixture into the flour mixture until well combined
4. Cook the batter into the iron waffle
5. Remove and serve

SUNBUTTER AND JELLY SMOOTHIE

Serves: 4
Prep Time: 10 Minutes
Cook Time: 30 Minutes
Total Time: 40 Minutes

INGREDIENTS

- 1 cup strawberries
- 1 medjool date
- 1 tablespoon sunflower seed butter
- pinch ground cinnamon
- stevia

- nuts
- granola
- honey

DIRECTIONS

1. In a blender add all ingredients and blend until smooth
2. Pour into a glass, top with nuts and serve

MORNING STRAWBERRY SHAKE

Serves: *1*
Prep Time: *10* Minutes

Cook Time: *30* Minutes

Total Time: *20* Minutes

INGREDIENTS

- 1 banana
- 1 cup strawberries
- ½ cup orange juice

- 1 cup ice

DIRECTIONS

1. In a blender add all ingredients and blend until smooth
2. Pour into a glass and serve

FRENCH TOAST

Serves: 2
Prep Time: **10** Minutes

Cook Time: **20** Minutes

Total Time: **30** Minutes

INGREDIENTS

- ½ cup orange juice
- ½ cup brown sugar
- 1 tablespoon diary-free buttery spread
- 1 tsp vanilla extract
- 1 cup strawberries

- ½ cup unsweetened dairy-free milk beverage
- 1 egg
- 1 tsp ground cinnamon
- 3 slices bread
- ½ cup dairy-free granola

DIRECTIONS

1. In a saucepan add oil, vanilla, orange juice and sugar
2. Add strawberries, banana and stir over medium heat
3. Cook for 6-7 minutes
4. In a bowl whisk together egg, cinnamon and milk, dip bread slices into mixture and place on a grill, cool 1-2 minutes per side
5. Serve toast with strawberry sauce

AVOCADO KALE BOWL

Serves: **4**
Prep Time: **10** Minutes
Cook Time: **30** Minutes
Total Time: **40** Minutes

INGREDIENTS

- 1 cup Greek yogurt (diary free yogurt)
- 1 cup kale leaves
- ½ cup protein powder
- ½ cup water
- ¼ ripe avocado
- 1 tsp stevia
- 1 tablespoon fresh mint
- ¼ cup frozen berries
- 1 tsp almonds
- 1 tablespoon chia seeds

DIRECTIONS

1. Place all ingredients in a blender and blend until smooth
2. Pour mixture into a bowl and serve in the morning

LUNCH

RICE PAPER ROLLS

Serves: **4**

Prep Time: **10** Minutes

Cook Time: **15** Minutes

Total Time: **25** Minutes

INGREDIENTS

- 1 cucumber
- 1 red capsicum
- 1 carrot
- 1 avocado
- 2 oz. pea sprouts
- ¾ coriander
- ¾ cup mint
- 2 oz. peanuts
- 2 tablespoons chili sauce
- 1 tablespoon soy sauce
- 2 tablespoons lime juice

DIRECTIONS

1. Place all the vegetables on a plate
2. In a bowl mix chili sauce, lime juice and soy sauce
3. Some one rice paper roll in a bowl of water and then place vegetables on the wrapper
4. Fold up the bottom of the wrapped, and roll u to enclose filling
5. Place on a tray, serve with dipping sauce

CHICKEN NOODLE SALAD

Serves: **4**

Prep Time: **10** Minutes

Cook Time: **30** Minutes

Total Time: **40** Minutes

INGREDIENTS

- 1 lb. tenderloins
- 2 oz. rice noodle
- 1 carrot
- 1 celery stalk
- 1 cucumber

- ¼ capsicum
- 1 tablespoon peanuts

DRESSING
- 1 onion
- 1 garlic clove
- ½ cup soy sauce
- ½ cup rice vinegar
- 1 tsp sugar
- 1 tsp sesame oil

DIRECTIONS

1. Place all dressing ingredients in a jar and mix well
2. In a bowl place all salad ingredients and mix well
3. Pour dressing over salad and serve

SHREDDED SWEET POTATO HASH BROWNS

Serves: **2**
Prep Time: **10** minutes
Cook Time: **30** minutes
Total Time: **40** minutes

INGREDIENTS

- 7 oz. sweet potatoes
- 3 tablespoons butter
- 1 tablespoon dried sage
- 1/8 tablespoon black pepper
- 1/8 tablespoon salt

DIRECTIONS

1. Shred the potatoes and place them in a strainer.
2. Use a rubber spatula and press the excess water.
3. Place the potatoes on a paper towel and pat as dry as possible.
4. Put the potatoes in a bowl and add sage, salt and pepper.
5. Place the butter in a skillet over high heat.
6. When the butter is melted add the potatoes.
7. Toss well for 5 minutes and gather them together into two piles.
8. Cook the potatoes slowly.
9. Cook on each side for 3 minutes.

SPAGHETTI WITH MEATBALLS

Serves: **2**

Prep Time: **10** minutes

Cook Time: **35** minutes

Total Time: **45** minutes

INGREDIENTS

- 4 quarts' water
- 5 meatballs
- ½ tomato sauce
- ½ ounces Parmigiano-Reggiano
- 2 ounces' spaghetti noodles

DIRECTIONS

1. In a large pot add water to high heat
2. Add spaghetti noodles
3. Add the meatballs and tomato sauce in a medium sauce pan while the pasta is cooking
4. Remove the noodles and allow them to drain
5. Place the noodles in the sauce with the meatballs

BEAN SOUP

Serves: **4**

Prep Time: **10** Minutes

Cook Time: **230** Minutes

Total Time: **240** Minutes

INGREDIENTS

- 2 cups beans
- 1/2 tsp salt
- 2 cups chicken broth
- 7 cups water
- 2 tsp sauce
- ½ 10-ounce package onions
- 2 clove garlic
- 3 bay leaves
- ½ tsp dried rosemary
- 1 tsp dried sage
- 2 tsp dried thyme

DIRECTIONS

1. Place the bean mixture in a pot with the rest of ingredients

2. Cook over medium heat until the soup boils
3. Reduce the heat and simmer for 3-4 hours
4. When ready remove from heat and serve

HOMEMADE CHICKEN NUGGETS

Serves: **4**

Prep Time: **10** Minutes

Cook Time: **30** Minutes

Total Time: **40** Minutes

INGREDIENTS

- 1 lbs. chicken breast
- 2 small eggs
- ¼ tsp garlic powder
- ¼ tsp salt
- ¼ cup breadcrumbs
- 1 ½ cups cauliflower

DIRECTIONS

1. Preheat oven to 325 F and place a baking tray in
2. In a bowl mix garlic powder, salt and egg and whisk together
3. In another bowl mix cauliflower and breadcrumbs, dip the chicken into the mixture
4. Bake for 20-25 minutes on each side

GRILLED VEGETABLES

Serves: 4

Prep Time: 10 Minutes

Cook Time: 10 Minutes

Total Time: 20 Minutes

INGREDIENTS

- 1 tablespoon olive oil
- ¼ tsp salt
- 2 bell peppers
- 1 bunch asparagus
- 2 small zucchini
- 1 tablespoon rice vinegar

- 1 tablespoon oregano
- 1 eggplant

DIRECTIONS

1. In a bowl whisk salt, oregano, vinegar and olive oil
2. Place the vegetables into a bowl
3. Place vegetables on a grill
4. Cook eggplant and zucchini pieces for 5-6 minutes per side
5. Toss asparagus and cool for 4-5 minutes
6. Transfer to a plate and serve when ready

PORK KEBABS

Serves: 8

Prep Time: 10 Minutes

Cook Time: 15 Minutes

Total Time: 25 Minutes

INGREDIENTS

- ½ cup fresh basil
- 22 red globe grapes
- ¼ Tsp allspice
- 1 lb. pork loin chop
- 1 tsp cumin
- ¼ tsp cardamom
- ¼ tsp salt
- 2 tsp fenugreek seeds
- ¼ black pepper

DIRECTIONS

1. In a bowl mix cumin, cardamom, salt, pepper, fenugreek and set aside
2. Cut the pork and sprinkle the mixture onto the pork cubes and stir until well coated
3. For each kebab slide a cube of pork into the skewer and alternate with basil wrapped grapes
4. Preheat the grill and cook for 10-15 minutes

TUNA PASTA SALAD

Serves: **4**

Prep Time: **10** Minutes

Cook Time: **30** Minutes

Total Time: **40** Minutes

INGREDIENTS

- 3 cups bow tie pasta
- 1 cup cherry tomatoes
- 1 tablespoon olive oil
- 2 tablespoons wine vinegar
- 1 tsp mustard
- ¼ cup parsley
- 1 tin tuna

DIRECTIONS

1. Place all ingredients in a bowl and mix well
2. Serve when ready

ROASTED CHICKPEAS

Serves: *4*

Prep Time: *10* Minutes

Cook Time: *30* Minutes

Total Time: *40* Minutes

INGREDIENTS

- 2 cans chickpeas
- 1 tsp olive oil
- 1 tsp salt
- 1 tsp pepper
- 1 tsp thyme
- 1 tsp rosemary

DIRECTIONS

1. Preheat oven to 350 F
2. Line an oven tray with baking paper, toss chickpeas in salt, pepper and oil
3. Pour mixture over baking paper and roast for 20-25 minutes
4. Remove and serve

MEDITERRANEAN GRILLED EGGPLANT SALAD

Serves: **6**

Prep Time: **35** Minutes

Cook Time: **20** Minutes

Total Time: **55** Minutes

INGREDIENTS

- ¾ Tsp salt
- ¼ Tsp black pepper
- 2 Tsp olive oil
- 2 ¾ lbs eggplant
- ½ cup mint leaves
- ¼ cup scallion greens
- 2 red bell pepper
- 2 tomato
- ¼ cup pine nuts
- ½ red pepper flakes
- 3 Tsp lemon juice
- 1/8 Tsp paprika

DIRECTIONS

1. In a skillet toast pine nuts over medium heat and stir frequently for 5 minutes
2. Halve and seed the red peppers, cut the eggplant and gill them over medium heat for 15-20 minutes
3. Transfer to a bowl and add scallion greens, lemon juice, tomato, olive oil, salt, paprika and red pepper flakes
4. Toss to combine ingredients and serve!

BAKED SALMON WITH ALMOND FLAXSEED CRUMBS

Serves: 5

Prep Time: 15 Minutes

Cook Time: 35 Minutes

Total Time: 50 Minutes

INGREDIENTS

- 1/8 tsp black pepper
- ¼ cup minced scallion greens
- ½ cup bread crumbs
- ¼ tsp thyme leaves

- 2 tsp olive oil
- 2 tsp lemon zest
- 1 ½ lbs. salmon
- ¼ cup whole almonds
- 3 tsp flaxseeds
- ¼ tsp salt

DIRECTIONS

1. Preheat the oven to 400 F and line a baking sheet
2. In a blender add flaxseeds and almonds and blend, move to a bowl and add bread crumbs, pepper, thyme, scallions, salt and lemon zest
3. Place the fish on the baking dish and brush it with garlic oil and sprinkle with salt
4. Bake it for 20-25 minutes

COLESLAW WITH TERIYAKI CHICKEN

Serves: 5
Prep Time: 50 Minutes
Cook Time: 15 Minutes

Total Time: 65   Minutes

INGREDIENTS

- 4 tsp reduced sodium soy sauce
- ¼ cup sesame oil
- ½ cup sliced scallion greens
- 4 tsp rice vinegar
- 3 tsp sugar
- 3 tsp ginger roots
- 1 tsp sesame seeds
- 1 8-ounce can water chestnuts
- 1 12-ounce shredded cabbage
- 2 carrots
- 1 ¾ lbs. chicken breasts
- ¼ tsp salt
- 1 ½ tsp canola oil
- ½ red bell pepper

DIRECTIONS

1. In a bowl add pepper, carrots, scallions and cabbage
2. In a bowl whisk sugar, soy sauce, rice vinegar, sesame oil and ginger
3. Whisk them and remove a quarter and pour the remaining dressing over the vegetables
4. Let the coleslaw marinate and stir, meanwhile slice chicken breast and sprinkle with salt
5. In a skillet add canola oil over medium heat

TOMATO SOUP

Serves: **1**

Prep Time: **10** minutes

Cook Time: **45** minutes

Total Time: **55** minutes

INGREDIENTS

- 1-quart homemade tomato sauce
- 1 can coconut milk
- 2 tablespoons minced fresh basil
- 1 tablespoons honey
- salt
- 1 cup cheese

DIRECTIONS

1. In a soup pot pour coconut milk and heat over high heat, add tomato sauce, honey, basil and salt
2. Simmer for 10-15 minutes
3. Preheat the oven to 425 F
4. Place a piece of parchment paper onto a baking sheet
5. Place small piles of cheese on the baking sheet, the cheese will melt down and spread

6. Place it in the oven for 5-10 minutes
7. Remove the crisps from the oven onto a plate and let it cool for 1-2 minutes

CHICKEN EGG DROP SOUP

Serves: 2
Prep Time: **10** minutes
Cook Time: **30** minutes
Total Time: **40** minutes

INGREDIENTS

- 7 cups chicken broth
- 2 chicken breasts
- 3 baby bok choy (chopped)
- ½ piece ginger
- 1 tablespoon coconut Aminos
- 2 eggs

DIRECTIONS

1. In a sauce pan boil he chicken, slice the chicken breasts and add in the sauce pan to boil, stir for 4-5 minutes
2. While boiling add bok choy and stir frequently for 4-5 minutes
3. Whisk the eggs, stir until they are cooked through
4. Add ladle, scallions and coconut aminos into bowls for serving

INDIAN KEBABS

Serves: **3**
Prep Time: **10** minutes
Cook Time: **15** minutes
Total Time: **25** minutes

INGREDIENTS

- 1 lb. ground beef
- 1 egg
- 2 tablespoons fresh ginger
- ½ tablespoon cinnamon
- ¼ tablespoon cloves

- ¼ cup chopped cilantro
- ¼ cup chopped mint
- salt

DIRECTIONS

1. Combine all the ingredients together and when ready roll the meat onto skewers
2. Cook grilled on your barbeque for 10-15 o each side
3. Remove, let it cool for 1-2 minutes and serve

BUTTERNUT SQUASH SOUP

Serves: 2
Prep Time: 10 minutes
Cook Time: 50 minutes
Total Time: 60 minutes

INGREDIENTS

- 1 tablespoon coconut oil
- ¼ tablespoons ginger
- 2 6" stalks of lemon grass

- 4 kaffir lime leaves
- 1 large butternut squash
- 1 cup home-made chicken broth
- salt

DIRECTIONS

1. In a pot add kaffir, lemon grass, ginger and coconut oil over low heat
2. Cook until softened for about 20 minutes
3. Add butternut squash cubes and stir until cubes are coted
4. Stir in chicken broth and cover with a lid and cook until squash is tender for 30 minutes
5. Taste and adjust with salt and pepper

ROASTED GARLIC

Serves: 2
Prep Time: **10** Minutes

Cook Time: **10** Minutes

Total Time: **20** Minutes

INGREDIENTS

- 1 head garlic
- 1 tablespoon olive oil

DIRECTIONS

1. Preheat oven to 375 F
2. Ove the garlic drizzle the olive oil and add to the pan
3. Roast for 15-20 minutes and remove from the oven
4. Let it cool and serve

TURMERIC FRIED EGG

Serves: *1*
Prep Time: *5* Minutes
Cook Time: *5* Minutes
Total Time: *10* Minutes

INGREDIENTS

- ½ Tbs avocado oil
- 2 eggs

- 1 Tsp turmeric

DIRECTIONS

1. Heat a skillet.
2. Add the avocado oil and turmeric.
3. Crack the eggs into the skillet and turn the heat to low.
4. Cook a few minutes.
5. Serve immediately.

FAJITAS WITH BASIL SAUCE

Serves: 2
Prep Time: **10** Minutes

Cook Time: **20** Minutes

Total Time: **30** Minutes

INGREDIENTS

- ½ cup quinoa
- 1 cup water

- ½ cup onion
- 1 tablespoon parsley
- 1 tsp lemon zest
- 6 tortillas
- 1 can cannellini beans
- 1 pint cheery tomatoes
- 1 cucumber

Basil sauce
- 8 tomatillos
- 2 tablespoons cannellini beans
- 1 cucumber
- 1 tablespoon almond butter
- 3 basil leaves

DIRECTIONS

1. Hold tortilla over flame to low heat for 3-4 seconds each side
2. Cook quinoa for 10-15 minutes and remove form heat
3. Puree the basil sauce ingredients in a blender
4. Season with salt and pepper and serve

DINNER

POT ROAST

Serves: **6**

Prep Time: **40** minutes

Cook Time: **210** minutes

Total Time: **250** minutes

INGREDIENTS

- 1 tablespoon dried sage
- 3 tablespoons olive oil
- 3 tablespoons bottom round
- 1 cup water
- 2 bay leaves
- 2 lbs. white potatoes
- 1 lb. carrots
- 1 tablespoon salt
- 2 large onions1
- ¼ black pepper

DIRECTIONS

1. **Preheat the oven to 225 F**

2. Add oil in a Dutch to medium heat
3. Sear the meat on each side for 2-5 minutes
4. Add sage, pepper, salt, bay leaves and onion and stir
5. Place the pot in the oven and let it roast for 3 hours
6. Remove the pan and also the onions and the liquid and place them in a blender
7. Add the potatoes and carrots and return the pot to the oven for 60-80 minutes
8. Remove the roast from the oven and add the pureed onions and stir

ROSEMARY GRILLED LAMB CHOPS

Serves: *4*

Prep Time: *15* Minutes

Cook Time: *100* Minutes

Total Time: *115* Minutes

INGREDIENTS

- 4 Tbs olive oil
- 4 Tbs rosemary leaves
- 6 lamb chops

- 3 Tsp sea salt
- 2 cloves garlic
- A pinch cayenne pepper

DIRECTIONS

1. Peel and chop the garlic.
2. Pulse the rosemary, garlic, oil and the spices in a food processor.
3. Marinate the lamb chops in the mixture for at least 1 hour.
4. Remove from the fridge and set aside for 20 minutes.
5. Heat a pan over medium heat.
6. Sear the lamb chops for 2 minutes.
7. Flip over and cook for another 3 minutes.
8. Allow to rest for 5 minutes and serve.

ORANGE GLAZED HAM

Serves: 4
Prep Time: 45 Minutes
Cook Time: 65 Minutes

Total Time: *110* Minutes

INGREDIENTS

- 6 whole whole cloves
- 8 lbs ham
- 1 cinnamon stick
- 1 cup sucanat
- ½ tsp black peppercorns
- 6 oranges

DIRECTIONS

1. Preheat the oven to 350F.
2. Juice the oranges and zest one.
3. Break the cinnamon stick
4. Mix the orange juice, sucanat, peppercorns, orange zest, cloves and cinnamon pieces in a saucepan over heat.
5. Stir and allow to simmer for 20 minutes.
6. Remove the skin and ½ of fay from the ham.
7. Place the ham in a roasting pan.
8. Bake for 1 hour, basting every 20 minutes with the sauce.
9. Allow to rest for 15 minutes, then serve.

ROAST LEG OF LAMB

Serves: **8**

Prep Time: **20** minutes

Cook Time: **100** minutes

Total Time: **120** minutes

INGREDIENTS

- 2 lbs. boneless leg of lamb
- 1/3 chicken broth
- 1 tablespoon butter
- ¼ black pepper
- 2 tablespoon oregano
- 1/3 salt
- 1 tablespoon olive oil

DIRECTIONS

1. Preheat the oven to 350 F
2. Trim the excess fat from the outside of the lamb
3. Sprinkle the leg with the oregano leaves
4. Roll the leg up
5. Heat a large skillet over high heat
6. When the skillet is hot and add the lamb

7. Sear and then turn to each side
8. Roast the lamb for 40 minutes
9. Place the skillet over high heat and add the chicken broth
10. Add the remaining ¼ teaspoon salt and whisk together

MUSHROOM PIZZA

Serves: 2
Prep Time: *10* Minutes
Cook Time: *30* Minutes
Total Time: *40* Minutes

INGREDIENTS

- 2 button mushrooms
- ½ red onion
- 1 lemon juiced
- 1 tablespoon parsley
- ½ cup ground flax seeds
- 2 tablespoons olive oil

- 1 cup almonds whole
- 1 cup cashews whole
- 1 carrot

DIRECTIONS

1. Preheat oven to 375 F and place a baking sheet
2. In food processor place all the ingredients and blend for 8-10 minutes
3. Pour the mixture on the baking sheet and bake for 15-20 minutes until golden
4. Remove from the oven and serve

GRAIN FREE FAJITAS

Serves: 3
Prep Time: **10** Minutes
Cook Time: **10** Minutes
Total Time: **20** Minutes

INGREDIENTS

- 1 tablespoon avocado oil

- 3 carrots
- 3 large nori sheets
- 1 tomato
- 1 tablespoon fresh cilantro
- 1 red pepper
- 1 green bell pepper
- 1 while onion
- 1 jalapeno

DIRECTIONS

1. In a skillet sauce avocado oil, onion, jalapeno, white onion, salt and pepper for 6-7 minutes
2. Remove from heat and place mixture in a bowl
3. Sauté carrots with pepper and salt for 5-6 minutes
4. Combine coconut milk with curry powder and combine with red onion, sea s alt and pepper
5. Lay the nori sheets and top with pepper mixture and carrots and drizzle with coconut milk

FISH TACOS

Serves: **4**

Prep Time: **10** Minutes

Cook Time: **30** Minutes

Total Time: **40** Minutes

INGREDIENTS

- 8 fish fingers
- ¼ cabbage
- tacos
- guacamole
- 2 avocados
- salt
- coriander
- juice of 1 lime

Salsa
- 2 cherry tomatoes
- ½ onion
- 1 tablespoon vinegar
- 8 jalapeno slices
- juice 1 lime
- salt

Spicy mayo
- ½ cup mayo
- 1 tablespoon paprika
- ½ cup ketchup
- juice 1 lime

DIRECTIONS

1. For salsa add all the ingredients into a blender and blend until smooth, place into a bowl and set aside
2. Mash avocado with salt, lime juice and mix with coriander
3. Mix your spicy mayo in a bowl, heat your tacos and pour the mixture on the tacos
4. Serve when ready

AVOCADO SANDWICH

Serves: *1*
Prep Time: *10* Minutes
Cook Time: *10* Minutes
Total Time: *20* Minutes

INGREDIENTS

- 1 avocado
- juice of 1 lemon pinch of salt
- coriander
- 6 rashers of bacon
- 4 slices bread
- 2 eggs
- ¼ tablespoon hot sauce

DIRECTIONS

1. In a pan add bacon and cook over medium heat
2. In a bowl mix lemon juice, salt, avocado and coriander
3. Toss your bread in the pan and crack an egg into the bread (make a hole before)
4. Add the avocado mixture over the bread and top with bacon
5. Remove and serve

APPLE ROASTED PORK CHOPS

Serves: **2**

Prep Time: **10** Minutes

Cook Time: **40** Minutes

Total Time: **50** Minutes

INGREDIENTS

- 2 pork chops
- 1 tablespoon thyme
- couple of sage leaves
- 1 tablespoon olive oil
- 1 tsp salt
- 3 apples
- ½ can apple cider
- shallots

DIRECTIONS

1. **Preheat oven to 325 F**
2. **Slice shallots and add them into a frying pan over medium heat**

3. Season pork chops with pepper and salt
4. Throw thyme in the pan, add pork chops and cook each side
5. Throw apples and cider
6. Put the pan in the oven for 30 minutes
7. Remove and serve

ROASTED EGGPLANT

Serves: **4**

Prep Time: **10** Minutes

Cook Time: **40** Minutes

Total Time: **50** Minutes

INGREDIENTS

- 2 eggplants
- 1 tablespoon olive oil
- 5 olives
- 2 cups canned cannellini
- 1 anchovy fillets
- 1 tablespoon lemon juice

- 1 tsp salt
- 1 cloves garlic
- ¼ chopped fresh parsley
- 2 dried tomatoes

DIRECTIONS

1. **Roast the eggplant in oven at 375 F for 40 minutes**
2. **In a blender add garlic and eggplant and add olive oil, parsley, tomato, beans, olives and lemon juice**
3. **Blend mixture until smooth remove and serve**

SPINACH SPREAD

Serves: 4

Prep Time: 10 Minutes

Cook Time: 20 Minutes

Total Time: 30 Minutes

INGREDIENTS

- 2 tsp canola oil

- ½ tsp lemon zest
- ½ tsp pepper
- ¼ grated nutmeg
- ½ cup water
- 2 10-ounce packages frozen spinach
- 1-ounce parmesan cheese
- 1 cup cottage cheese
- 2 tablespoons lemon juice
- 1 cup onion
- 2 cloves garlic

DIRECTIONS

1. In a skillet heat oil over medium heat and add garlic and onion
2. Cook for 7-8 minutes an add water and spinach
3. Transfer mixture in a blender and add parmesan cheese, lemon juice, cottage cheese, pepper, lemon zest, nutmeg, salt and puree until smooth
4. Refrigerate at least 4h before serving

LENTIL HUMMUS

Serves: **4**

Prep Time: **10** Minutes

Cook Time: **30** Minutes

Total Time: **40** Minutes

INGREDIENTS

- 1 15-ounce can lentils
- ¼ tsp salt
- ¼ ground cumin
- ¼ cup water
- ½ cup sesame tahini
- 1 clove garlic
- ¼ cup olive oil
- 2 tablespoons lemon juice

DIRECTIONS

1. Mix all the ingredients except water in a blender and blend until smooth
2. Remove and serve

LEMON ROSEMARY CHICKEN

Serves: **4**

Prep Time: **10** Minutes

Cook Time: **30** Minutes

Total Time: **40** Minutes

INGREDIENTS

- 4 6oz. boneless chicken breast
- 2 tsp olive oil
- 1 tsp lemon pepper seasoning
- 1 tsp salt
- 2 lemons
- fresh rosemary
- 1 cup chicken broth
- ½ tsp garlic

DIRECTIONS

1. Preheat oven to 350 F
2. Brush chicken with olive oil and sprinkle with lemon seasoning
3. In a baking dish place chicken with rosemary and top with lemon slices

4. Bake for 20-25 minutes or until golden brown
5. In a saucepan mix rosemary with chicken broth and garlic
6. Serve mixture with chicken and garnish with lemon slices

SHRIMP SKEWERS WITH GARLIC

Serves: 3

Prep Time: 10 Minutes

Cook Time: 25 Minutes

Total Time: 35 Minutes

INGREDIENTS

- 2 oz. shrimp
- 2 dried guindilla peppers
- 1 clove garlic
- 1 tsp parsley
- ¼ cup olive oil
- salt
- pepper

DIRECTIONS

1. Skewer shrimp on bamboo skewers
2. Mix the remaining ingredients and pour the mixture over the skewers and marinate
3. Season with salt and pepper and serve

PICKLED BEETS

Serves: **4**

Prep Time: **10** Minutes

Cook Time: **60** Minutes

Total Time: **70** Minutes

INGREDIENTS

- 1 bunch beets
- ¼ cup cider vinegar
- ¼ cup water
- 1 onion
- 1 clove garlic
- ¼ tsp salt

- 1 tablespoon honey

DIRECTIONS

1. In a saucepan add the beets and water and boil on high heat for 40-45 minutes
2. Drain and peel the beets and slice them
3. Put the beets back in the saucepan and add the rest of the ingredients except honey
4. Cook for 10-15 minutes
5. Remove from heat and add honey

AVOCADO DIP

Serves: 2
Prep Time: 5 Minutes

Cook Time: 5 Minutes

Total Time: 10 Minutes

INGREDIENTS

- 2 avocados
- ¼ cup mayonnaise

- ¼ tsp salt
- ½ tsp sesame oil
- 1 clove garlic
- 1 tablespoon chives

DIRECTIONS

1. Place all the ingredients in a blender and blend until smooth
2. Remove and serve

GREEN BEANS WITH MUSHROOMS

Serves: **4**
Prep Time: **10** Minutes
Cook Time: **10** Minutes
Total Time: **20** Minutes

INGREDIENTS

- ½ lbs. green beans
- 1 shallot
- ¼ tsp thyme leaves

- ¼ tsp basil
- 1 tsp cider vinegar
- 1 clove garlic
- 3-ounces mushrooms
- ¼ tsp salt
- 1 tablespoon almonds
- 1 tablespoon olive oil

DIRECTIONS

1. Steam the beans for 4-5 minutes
2. In a pan add olive oil and shallot and sauce over medium heat for 2-3 minutes
3. Add garlic, mushrooms and green beans and sauté for 2-3 minutes
4. Stir in thyme, salt, basil and vinegar
5. Sprinkle sliced almonds over and serve

BUTTERNUT SQUASH WITH APPLES

Serves: **10**

Prep Time: **10** Minutes

Cook Time: **45** Minutes

Total Time: **55** Minutes

INGREDIENTS

- 12 oz. bacon
- 1 tsp salt
- 1 tsp allspice
- zest of one lime
- ½ tsp pepper
- 2 oz. shallots
- 2 lb. organic butternut squash
- 3 apples
- 1 cup cranberries
- 1 tablespoon sage

DIRECTIONS

1. Preheat oven to 375 F
2. In a skillet add shallots, bacon and cook until bacon is crisp

3. In a bowl toss squash, apples, cranberries, sage, salt, allspice, lime zest and white pepper
4. Transfer the mixture to a baking dish and bake for 45 minutes
5. Garnish with sage and serve

MEAT MARINADE

Serves: **4**

Prep Time: **10** Minutes

Cook Time: **30** Minutes

Total Time: **40** Minutes

INGREDIENTS

- ¼ cup vinegar
- ½ tsp salt
- 2 tablespoons soy sauce
- ¼ cup olive oil
- 2 tablespoons water
- 2 cloves garlic

DIRECTIONS

1. In a bowl add all the ingredients and mix well
2. Refrigerate marinade

RED QUINOA

Serves: **4**

Prep Time: **10** Minutes

Cook Time: **35** Minutes

Total Time: **45** Minutes

INGREDIENTS

- 2 tsp olive oil
- ½ tsp salt
- 1 cup water
- 1 cup red quinoa
- 1 stalks red chard

DIRECTIONS

1. In a saucepan add salt, olive oil and water
2. Stir in quinoa, bring to boil and simmer for 12-15 minutes
3. Stir in red chard and simmer, after 5-6 minutes add more water and bring to boil
4. Remove and serve

SNACKS & DESERT

ACAI SMOOTHIE

Serves: **1**

Prep Time: **5** Minutes

Cook Time: **5** Minutes

Total Time: **10** Minutes

INGREDIENTS

- 1 cup blueberries
- 1 avocado
- 1 tablespoon flaxseed
- 1 tablespoon hemp hearts
- 1 tablespoon chia seeds
- 1 tablespoon acai powder
- 1 scoop vanilla protein powder
- ½ cup water

DIRECTIONS

1. In a blender place all ingredients and blend until smooth

2. Pour smoothie in a glass and serve

PROTEIN SMOOTHIE

Serves: 1
Prep Time: 5 Minutes
Cook Time: 5 Minutes
Total Time: 10 Minutes

INGREDIENTS

- ½ cup gluten-free oats
- 1 banana
- 1 tablespoon cashew butter
- 1 tablespoon hemp seeds
- 1 tsp cocoa powder
- 1 tsp maple syrup
- ½ tsp vanilla extract
- ice cubes

DIRECTIONS

1. In a blender place all ingredients and blend until smooth
2. Pour smoothie in a glass and serve

GOJI SMOOTHIE

Serves: *1*

Prep Time: *5* Minutes

Cook Time: *5* Minutes

Total Time: *10* Minutes

INGREDIENTS

- Zest of 1 orange
- 1 orange
- 1 banana
- ½ cup goji berries
- 1 tablespoon hemp seeds
- 1 tablespoon chia seeds
- ice cubes

DIRECTIONS

1. In a blender place all ingredients and blend until smooth
2. Pour smoothie in a glass and serve

AVOCADO BLUEBERRY SMOOTHIE

Serves: 1
Prep Time: 5 Minutes
Cook Time: 5 Minutes
Total Time: 10 Minutes

INGREDIENTS

- 1 cup blueberries
- 1 cup frozen mango
- ½ avocado
- 1 tablespoon chia seeds
- 1 tsp Maca powder2
- 1 tablespoon honey

DIRECTIONS

1. In a blender place all ingredients and blend until smooth
2. Pour smoothie in a glass and serve

VEGAN SHAKE

Serves: **1**

Prep Time: **5** Minutes

Cook Time: **5** Minutes

Total Time: **10** Minutes

INGREDIENTS

- 1 cup blueberries
- ½ cup strawberries
- ½ banana
- ½ avocado
- 1 tsp hemp seeds

DIRECTIONS

1. In a blender place all ingredients and blend until smooth
2. Pour smoothie in a glass and serve

PEACH SMOOTHIE

Serves: *1*

Prep Time: *5* Minutes

Cook Time: *5* Minutes

Total Time: *10* Minutes

INGREDIENTS

- 1 cup unsweetened almond milk
- ½ cup frozen sliced peaches
- ½ cup protein powder
- handful of ice

DIRECTIONS

1. In a blender place all ingredients and blend until smooth
2. Pour smoothie in a glass and serve

MANGO SMOOTHIE

Serves: **1**

Prep Time: **5** Minutes

Cook Time: **5** Minutes

Total Time: **10** Minutes

INGREDIENTS

- 1 mango
- 1 tablespoon honey
- 1 tablespoon oat
- ¼ water
- ice cubes

DIRECTIONS

1. In a blender place all ingredients and blend until smooth
2. Pour smoothie in a glass and serve

PINEAPPLE SMOOTHIE

Serves: **1**

Prep Time: **5** Minutes

Cook Time: **5** Minutes

Total Time: **10** Minutes

INGREDIENTS

- 1 cup unsweetened almond milk
- ½ cup frozen sliced pineapple
- ½ cup protein powder
- handful of ice

DIRECTIONS

1. **In a blender place all ingredients and blend until smooth**
2. **Pour smoothie in a glass and serve**

BEERY SMOOTHIE

Serves: **1**

Prep Time: **5** Minutes

Cook Time: **5** Minutes

Total Time: **10** Minutes

INGREDIENTS

- 1 cup unsweetened almond milk
- ½ cup frozen sliced berries
- ½ cup protein powder
- handful of ice

DIRECTIONS

1. **In a blender place all ingredients and blend until smooth**
2. **Pour smoothie in a glass and serve**

STRAWBERRY SMOOTHIE

Serves: **1**

Prep Time: **5** Minutes

Cook Time: **5** Minutes

Total Time: **10** Minutes

INGREDIENTS

- 1 cup vanilla almond milk(unsweetened)
- ½ cup oats
- 1 cup strawberries
- 1 scoop protein powder

DIRECTIONS

1. In a blender place all ingredients and blend until smooth
2. Pour smoothie in a glass and serve

BLUEBERRY DESSERT

Serves: **4**

Prep Time: **10** Minutes

Cook Time: **20** Minutes

Total Time: **30** Minutes

INGREDIENTS

- 1 apple
- ½ tsp cloves
- ½ cup orange juice
- 2 tablespoons honey
- ½ cup water
- ½ tsp ginger
- blueberries
- ½ tsp cinnamon

CRUST

- ½ cup almond flour
- 1 egg
- 1 tsp honey
- ¼ tsp cinnamon

DIRECTIONS

1. Preheat oven to 325 F
2. In a saucepan add water, orange juice and honey
3. Add apples into the saucepan and simmer for 10 minutes on low heat
4. In a bowl mix all ingredients for crust
5. Spoon dough into the middle of a baking sheet
6. Bake for 9-10 minutes and remove from the oven
7. Spread honey over the crust and place blueberries over apples and sprinkle with cinnamon

BANANA BREAKFAST CAKES

Serves: 4
Prep Time: 10 Minutes
Cook Time: 40 Minutes
Total Time: 50 Minutes

INGREDIENTS

- 1 cup peanut butter
- ½ cup applesauce

- ½ cup walnuts
- ½ almonds
- ½ tsp salt
- 1 egg
- 2 bananas
- ½ cup raisins
- 1 cup almond flour
- 1 tsp baking soda

DIRECTIONS

1. Preheat oven to 325
2. Line a muffin pan with baking cups
3. In a bowl add almond flour, baking soda, peanut butter and salt and mix well
4. Add eggs, applesauce, mashed bananas and mix well
5. Beat mixture using a blender for 4-5 minutes
6. Stir in raisins and nuts
7. Pour batter into baking cups and bake for 35 minutes
8. Remove and serve

CHERRY PEACH BOATS

Serves: **6**

Prep Time: **10** Minutes

Cook Time: **35** Minutes

Total Time: **45** Minutes

INGREDIENTS

- 5 peaches
- ½ cup cherries
- ½ cup blueberries
- 2 tablespoons pecans
- 1 tsp honey
- ½ tsp cinnamon

DIRECTIONS

1. Preheat oven to 375 F
2. Chop the flesh from peaches and reserve it in a mixing bowl
3. Slice cherries and remove pits, place cherries in a mixing bowl
4. Add pecans, honey, blueberries, cinnamon and stir to combine all ingredients

5. Sprinkle with cinnamon and place the mixture in the oven for 15 minutes
6. Remove and serve

CARROT CAKE

Serves: **6**

Prep Time: **10** Minutes

Cook Time: **40** Minutes

Total Time: **50** Minutes

INGREDIENTS

- 1 box cake mix
- 1 cup grated carrots
- ½ cup water
- 2 eggs
- ½ cup vegetable oil
- ½ cup raisins
- ¼ cup pineapple
- 1 tsp cinnamon
- ½ cup walnuts

DIRECTIONS

1. Preheat convection oven to 325 F or oven to 350 F
2. Brush a cake pan with butter and flour
3. In a bowl add all the ingredients and beat on low speed until everything is incorporated
4. Divided the batter into 2 pans and bake for 35 minutes or normal oven for 40 minutes
5. Remove and allow cakes to cook and serve

CHINESE ALMOND COOKIES

Serves: 6

Prep Time: 10 Minutes

Cook Time: 25 Minutes

Total Time: 35 Minutes

INGREDIENTS

- 2 cups flour
- ½ tsp salt
- 1 cup sugar
- 1 egg

- ½ cup almonds
- ½ tsp soda
- 1 tsp almond extract

DIRECTIONS

1. In a bowl sift sugar, soda, salt and flour
2. Add egg, almond extract and mix well
3. Shape dough into 1 inch balls and place on a cookie sheet
4. Bake at 300 F for 20 minutes
5. Remove and serve

PAPAYA MIX

Serves: 2
Prep Time: **10** Minutes
Cook Time: **10** Minutes
Total Time: **20** Minutes

INGREDIENTS

- 1 green papaya
- 1 carrot
- 1-inch fresh ginger
- 1 tablespoon sugar
- 1 tablespoon vinegar
- water
- ½ tablespoon fish sauce

DIRECTIONS

1. Mix sugar with vinegar, ginger and water
2. Mix well and stir into mix of papaya and carrot
3. Serve with different Vietnamese dishes

SUGAR CANE JUICE

Serves: 4
Prep Time: 10 Minutes
Cook Time: 30 Minutes
Total Time: 40 Minutes

INGREDIENTS

- 1 sugar cane stick
- 3 limes
- ice cubes

DIRECTIONS

1. Peel sugar cane, squeeze it and add limes
2. Serve with ice

FRUIT SALSA

Serves: **4**

Prep Time: **10** Minutes

Cook Time: **10** Minutes

Total Time: **20** Minutes

INGREDIENTS

- 1 tsp lime zest
- ½ cup lime juice

- 1 tablespoon sugar
- 2 cups watermelon
- 1 cucumber
- 1 mango
- 1 cup corn
- 1 red onion
- pepper

DIRECTIONS

1. In a bowl mix lime zest, juice, sugar and pepper
2. Add cucumber, mango, onion and the rest of ingredients and toss
3. Serve when ready

CRANBERRY SORBET

Serves: *4*

Prep Time: *10* Minutes

Cook Time: *10* Minutes

Total Time: *20* Minutes

INGREDIENTS

- 1 cup frozen cranberry
- 1 cup crushed ice
- 1 tablespoon lemon juice
- ½ cup water
- ½ cup sugar

DIRECTIONS

1. In a blender add all ingredients and blend until smooth
2. Place in a freezer for a couple of hours, remove and serve

CANDY GRAPES

Serves: *4*

Prep Time: *10* Minutes

Cook Time: *10* Minutes

Total Time: *20* Minutes

INGREDIENTS

- 1 box gelatin
- 1 cup water
- lemon juice

DIRECTIONS

1. Place gelatin into a bowl
2. Dip a toothpick in water and roll in mix
3. Place in fridge to chill
4. Remove and serve

THANK YOU FOR READING THIS BOOK!

Printed in Great Britain
by Amazon